Thirteen Hands

Carol Shields, with seven novels, two books of short stories, three books of poetry and four plays to her credit, has firmly established herself as one of Canada's finest writers, very much in the same league as Munro, Atwood or Gallant.

She is the past recipient of such prestigious awards as the Arthur Ellis Award (for *Swann: a literary mystery*) and the Marian Engel Award, as well as recently placing second in the 1992 U.K. Guardian Fiction Prize for her novel, *The Republic of Love*.

Carol Shields lives in Winnipeg, teaches at the University of Manitoba and has just completed a new novel.

Carol Shields

Thirteen Hands

a play in two acts

Blizzard Publishing • **Winnipeg**

Thirteen Hands first published 1993 by
Blizzard Publishing Inc.
73 Furby Street, Winnipeg, Canada R3C 2A2
© 1993 Carol Shields
Reprinted 1997.

Cover design by Scott Barham.
Printed in Canada.

Published with the assistance of
the Canada Council and the Manitoba Arts Council.

Canadian Cataloguing in Publication Data

Shields, Carol, 1935–
   Thirteen hands
   A play.
   ISBN 0-921368-30-5
I. Title.
PS8587.H46T45 1993   C812'.54   C93-098055-7
PR9199.3.S514T45 1993

For Kathleen Flaherty
with affection and with admiration

Thirteen Hands was first produced by Prairie Theatre Exchange, Winnipeg, on January 28, 1993, with the following cast:

EAST	Colleen Tillotson
NORTH	Linda Huffman
SOUTH	Karen Gartner
WEST	Nancy Drake

Director: Kathleen Flaherty
Set and Lighting Design: Douglas Paraschuk
Costume Design: Laara Cassells
Original Music Composed: Greg Lowe
Assistant Director: Kayla Gordon
Choreography: Brenda Gorlick
Stage Manager: Janet Remy
Assistant Stage Manager: Russell Bragg

Thirteen Hands was originally commissioned by Agassiz Theatre and workshopped by the Manitoba Association of Playwrights. It was read at the Tarragon Theatre early in 1990 and given a staged public reading. Later in the year the Manitoba Association of Playwrights again workshopped the play and provided a staged reading. In the spring of 1991 The Canadian Stage Company in Toronto workshopped and critiqued the play.

Many friends and colleagues have helped bring *Thirteen Hands* into existence. The playwright thanks Catherine Shields, Craig Walls, Laurie Lam, Urjo Kareda, Steven Schipper, Michael Springate, the Manitoba Association of Playwrights, the Canadian Stage Company and the Manitoba Arts Council for encouragement. George Toles and Chris Johnson offered invaluable suggestions on the text. Kathleen Flaherty, assisted by Kayla Gordon, directed the première production with flair and tact. Doug Paraschuk's set and lighting glowed with magic. Laara Cassell's costumes were evocative and witty. Greg Lowe's music left the audience humming. Nancy Mitchell gave expert bridge instruction. Actors Nancy Drake, Linda Huffman, Colleen Tillotson and Karen Gartner performed with grace and authority. And, finally, Janet Remy, as stage manager, kept track of the thousand details required to transform a two-dimensional manuscript into a three-dimensional theatrical experience.

Playwright's Note

For many years I've been interested in the lives of women, particularly those lives that have gone unrecorded. The last twenty or thirty years have seen, in literature and in theatre, the (partial) redemption of women artists and activists. But one group seems consistently overlooked: a group who, for historical reasons mainly, were caught between movements, the so called "blue rinse set," the "ladies of the club," the bridge club "biddies." There were (are) thousands of these women, millions in fact. I am reluctant to believe that their lives are wasted or lost. Something important goes on around a bridge table, a place where many women have felt most brilliantly alive.

Thirteen Hands attempts to valorize those lives. Two principal patterns of human behaviour play against each other: continuity and replacement.

Continuity is represented by the multi-generational range of the play and by the way women create and preserve history in their stories.

Replacement is the inevitability that all people face; in this play new faces appear around the table; a wife replaces one who dies, mothers are replaced by daughters and granddaughters. In *Thirteen Hands* the four founding members of the bridge club are all, one by one, replaced, but there is an ever-present yearning—expressed in the final scene—to return to that moment when the four original members sat down at a table in the early years of this century and began their lives.

The game of bridge is used literally and metaphorically in the play, and it is hoped that this doubleness is strengthened by the fact that the word "bridge" never appears.

Production Notes

It is hoped that the open structure of the play will permit directors a measure of flexibility, so that they can omit scenes or juggle their placement. It is taken for granted that geographical references be changed to suit particular audiences.

The play's various scenes shift back and forth between the naturalistic and the abstract mode. Suitable lighting can gesture toward, and enhance, these shifts.

Costumes are simple, a basic "slip" or "shift" is envisioned, the same colour in different styles, or perhaps the same style in differing colours. To the basic costume, a number of simple additions can be made: a string of pearls, aprons, sweaters, hats, corsages, and so forth. All costume changes can be made on stage if desired.

Scenes are separated by sound, by segments of recorded music, by live music (if possible), by the impromptu and informal singing of the actors themselves, or by a tape of women's voices talking and laughing, the actual words indistinct but a mood of conviviality conveyed.

All roles are written to be played by four women actors, indicated in the text as NORTH, EAST, SOUTH and WEST. It is possible, though, to stage the play using a much larger number of performers.

The action of *Thirteen Hands* takes place at the Martha Circle and other tables, 1920–1993.

Act One

(At rise: the stage is bare. A card table is folded against back wall, as are the utterly standard wooden folding chairs. At stage left is a dressing room equipped with dressing table, mirror, rack for clothes, bench. A bicycle leans against the wall. At far stage right is a lectern.

Tape of women laughing and talking. Four women at stage left are helping each other pin a corsage on each other's shoulder. Tape fades to music. They look at each other approvingly. Then enter and take their places at stage front, lining up awkwardly as though not sure of their place. They speak to each other and also to the audience.)

SOUTH: Ahem!

NORTH: Shouldn't we begin. *(Looks at watch.)*

WEST: Everyone ... *(She surveys audience.)* is assembled. I suggest we begin at once.

SOUTH: Allow me.

EAST: Well, actually it would make more sense if we—

SOUTH: What?

EAST: If we went alphabetically.

WEST: That puts me last.

NORTH: Does it matter to ... *(Waves in direction of audience.)* who comes first or last?

SOUTH: It's critical. Once you start getting lax about rules—

EAST: —you're in a different convention.

WEST: I hadn't thought of that, but of course you're right.

EAST: Ahem. To introduce myself, then, I'm East.

NORTH: *(Bowing.)* North here. And you must be—

SOUTH: Right you are. South. And to my right is—

WEST: West.

> *(They all shake hands, murmuring polite greetings.)*

SOUTH: *(Impatiently.)* Well?

WEST: I think that completes the formalities. Let's get right down to—

EAST: Something's missing. *(Holds up finger—idea!)*

NORTH: *(Pulling out cards, executing in-hand shuffle.)* I have the necessary ... wherewithal.

WEST: Shall we take our places? *(Looks around for table and chairs.)*

SOUTH: Isn't that what we're here for?

EAST: A good question.

SOUTH: I suggest we stop asking questions and get down to it.

NORTH: *(Persisting.)* Nevertheless, questions occur whether we ask them or not—

WEST: What questions?

EAST: Why we're here. What we're doing.

SOUTH: Is it really necessary—posing these kinds of questions?

EAST: There are those ... who may not ...

WEST: —comprehend who we are—

NORTH: —who doubt our ... seriousness, our—

EAST: —our essential value, to put it baldly.

SOUTH: *(Rising to argument.)* There *are* millions of us, after all. No, billions. That would mean ... as an estimate, that several hundred million hands are played every day—

WEST: Conservative estimate.

NORTH: Very.

SOUTH: Several million times each small act. *(Holds up card.)*

EAST: Impressive. And if you multiply that by the energy requirement, you find the result—

WEST: —equals—

SOUTH: Shhhhhh, listen.

(Voices may be either live or previously recorded.)

VOICE ONE [NORTH]: *(Reads in sepulchral tones.)* Opening lead—seven of clubs. Some contracts are extremely difficult to make. Here is one brilliantly played some years ago in a non-championship game in Winnipeg, Manitoba, where correct play produced twelve tricks. Six no-trump was bid, played and made by a certain Clara Wesley, widow of one Arthur Wesley, during a scheduled Tuesday night match. It was relatively easy for her to diagnose West's opening lead as either a singleton or a—*(Fades.)*

VOICE TWO [EAST]: *(Overtaking previous voice, speaking in teacherly manner, perhaps with echo.)*—one spade! This may appear to be an enormous underbid, but—

VOICE ONE: A little carelessness caused declarer to blow this deal, despite a very favourable lie of cards.

VOICE TWO: South was defeated because she squandered her entries to hand. She should have—*(Fades.)*

VOICE ONE: —should have postponed the drawing of trumps while—*(Fades.)*

VOICE TWO: Never stall unnecessarily. You confuse your—

VOICE ONE: The coolest nerves can be shaken by—

VOICE TWO: Steady does it when a single club ruff reveals—

VOICE ONE: Before deciding which way to take a two-way finesse, declarer must—

VOICE TWO: —at other times—

VOICE ONE: South can proceed with absolute confidence.

SOUTH: *(Breaking mood.)* Absolute confidence? Does such a thing exist?

WEST: It's a question of keeping track of things. Lists.

NORTH: Ace, kings, queens, ten, et cetera. Lists. You know how good we are at keeping—

(The rest of the scene is played at top speed.)

EAST: *(Counting on fingers.)* Carrots, potatoes, ground beef, sugar—

NORTH: June, August, October, December—

SOUTH: Piano lessons, dry cleaning, fire insurance—

WEST: 123 west 68th, 29 Portage Road, 935 Beverly Crescent—

NORTH: Five pounds six ounces; eight pounds, one ounce; six and a half—

SOUTH: Emily, Roberta, Alma, Alison, Izzie—

EAST: Aunt May, Uncle Si, Grandpa Muldoon—

WEST: Symphony, board meeting, lecture series, art gallery—

SOUTH: Canasta, bunko, ma-jong, scrabble—

EAST: Measles, chicken pox, diphtheria—

WEST: Seersucker, piquet, organdy, velveteen—

SOUTH: Chairs, umbrella, beach towels, thermos—

NORTH: Four ninety-five. Two dollars and fifty cents. Twelve dollars even—

SOUTH: Someone has to keep the lists.

NORTH: Of course they do.

SOUTH: Lard, shortening, baking powder—

NORTH: Galations, Ephesians, Philippians—

WEST: Lima, Buenos Aires, Mexico City—

EAST: Peanuts, pencils, tallies, ashtrays—

WEST: Tricks, trumps, books, hands—

EAST: There are variations. Schisms.

NORTH: Better not gone into, I think. Not here.

SOUTH: Time to go. Just one more thing before you're on your way. Can you give me a hand with this.

(She points to folded up card table. They set up the card table ceremonially to musical accompaniment. A loud beat as each leg is unfolded. There is a little fussing with the angle of the table, getting it just right, and then each places a chair in position.

Music: At stage left three women help the elderly CLARA [WEST] get ready for her entrance, assisting her with her dressing gown, putting her glasses on her nose, applying face powder, brushing her hair. One of them puts a lace cloth on card table. When CLARA enters, the other women sit on bench.

Light on CLARA as she enters from left, shuffling a little in her gown. At first she can't find the card table, walks by it, looks around, confused, then sees it. She rummages in her pockets and finds, finally, a deck of cards which she shuffles in her hand—the first sign of her mounting energy. CLARA then deals out cards into four hands, walking around the table as she does so, increasing her speed and energy until she achieves a sort of halting Jazz rhythm.)

CLARA: De-dum, de-dum, de-dum and ... de-dum. With a one and two and three and a four.

(She stops, kisses pack, blows on it for luck.)

And a little one, and a big one and a little one and a big one, here we round the dum-de-dum bush on a frosty Tuesday evening.

(She stops herself, listens, then continues.)

With a one and two and three and a four, *(Reversing herself.)* with a four and three and a two and a one. *(Pauses.)* With a—

(She lifts top cards, looks at it, considers putting it down, then changes her mind, mixing it into deck and vigorously reshuffling.)

For you and you ... and you ... and me. You, you, you and me. Ruth, Margot—ah, Margot—Doris,—and me. Ruthie, Margot, Doris and ... Clara.

(Stops abruptly, dizzy, sits down at one of the chairs.)

Clara. Clar-a.

(Cuts remaining deck and continues, dealing counter-clockwise.)

Clara. Doris, Margot, Ruth, Clar-a, Do-ris, Mar-got, Ruth-ie. Last round, ladies, for the-four-of-us. *(Picks up hand and briskly sorts.)* All right, gals, breast your cards. Whew. Well! And I felt lucky tonight. Just goes to show. Hmmmm.

(Puts hand face down on table, rises painfully and goes to pick up Doris's hand.)

Not bad at all. Not discouragingly bad. Playable. Eminently playable. With support, that is.

(Moves to Margot's chair and arranges her hand.)

Well, well! Length, strength, two queens, ace, gor-geous. *(Looks up at audience.)* Not that gorgeous was a word in Margot's vocabulary. Not Margot. *(Mimics.)* Tidy little spread, very tidy.

(Reaches across table to pick up and arrange Ruth's hand.)

Ruth. Ruth Sprague. Your luck's swung round tonight, my girl. Bid this with your usual verve, your well-tempered verve, that's what we used to say about your bidding, well tempered, and you'll sail home tonight on spades. Gorgeous spades.

(She starts playing hand and then stops, hearing kettle whistle.)
The kettle, and just when we were all getting a little dry. Thistles in the throat as Doris put it.

(She rises, shuffles off and is back quickly with a tea cup, addressing audience.)

I remember how it was when Ruth here got so sick. *(Pats back of chair.)* She started missing our Tuesday nights, some excuse or other, or else she'd have to go home early, pass up the dainties, tell us how she'd lost her appetite. Coconut squares, cherry slice, Rice Krispie bars, marshmallow melts—oh, the peculiar things we used to make!—she passed them up, shook her head, thank you just the same. And she'd get pooped out. Couldn't concentrate. One night, we couldn't get over it, she miscarded. Played the jack of diamonds when we all knew she had trump in her hand, clubs, I think it was. Well! There was this unholy silence. We didn't know where to look. She twigged at last. "Oh, my lord," she said, "just look what I've done, oh, for crying out loud."

She never did come right out and talk about … it. Just said, after she'd been to the hospital for tests, that things weren't right … down there. But the pain, oh the pain was something else. I saw her once, dropped in unexpectedly. She had this piece of old cloth, an old handkerchief of Rudy's, I think it was, and she was biting down on that. Of course that was toward the end.

It bothered me, seeing her like that, with a handkerchief jammed between her teeth. She was an attractive woman when she was young. Not pretty, but she could look queenly. She wore a hat well, we all agreed on that. But she shrank down. It's a fact that a human figure, seen on its own, is very small. She was the first of us to go—she would have been sixty that spring. Oh, they offered her morphine, here they said, take this, but no, not Ruthie, she didn't want to go all fuzzy and buzzy, she said. She was always one to pride herself on her brains—she'd been a stenographer, for two years, before she married, worked in an office, insurance—she wanted to keep alert, even when the pain was half way to killing her. Actually, though, it was Doris Veal, to give her credit, who said something had to be done for Ruthie when she was in such pain, going through H-E-double-hockey-sticks. We're her friends, Doris said, and if the family's not going to lift a finger, it's up to us. We've got to have a word with the doctor. Oh, that doctor. He was quite the boy, but he had a way about him that cheered you. We went to see him, the three of us, Doris, Margot Hetherling and myself. We drove over in Doris's Vauxhall, a cold March day, Doris was sucking one of her everlasting peppermints, I remember. I wore my new dressmaker suit and matching hat. We told the doctor outright—you've got to do something for Ruth Sprague, we said. He just looked at us hard—then he looked at us in a winking way—and he said, "Ladies, the only thing that'd help her is if you'd boil up a deck of cards and serve her the broth." *(Laughs.)* Anyway, he said, she won't last long with cancer of the uterus, no one does.

It hurt me to hear it said out loud. It affected me. But that doctor was right about Ruthie, she didn't last long.

> *(CLARA puts away cards, folds table cloth, straightens chairs. PEAKED CAP [NORTH], wearing a peaked cap, rides to centre stage on bicycle, ringing bell loudly.)*

CLARA: *(Looking up.)* Oh, it's you.

PEAKED CAP: I'm not interrupting?

CLARA: Not at all. *(Smoothing table cloth.)* We're all done for today.

PEAKED CAP: I brought the questionnaire.

CLARA: *(Glancing at paper.)* Oh, that, I didn't know it was time for that again.

PEAKED CAP: It won't take long. A few minutes.

CLARA: Well, let's get it over with then.

PEAKED CAP: *(Clearing throat, reaching for pencil, and reading.)* Question one. Do you, Clara Wesley, consider yourself a marginal person?

CLARA: Weellll, I suppose it depends on where the centre is.

PEAKED CAP: Shall I write that down?

CLARA: I don't know. I think someone else's already said it. And anyway, it might seem … disrespectful.

PEAKED CAP: That's my question. Are you given to making rude, forthright or disrespectful statements?

CLARA: Well, now, I don't know.

PEAKED CAP: *(Reading.)* When faced with a difficult question, do you say: "Well, now, I don't know"?

CLARA: Well now—

PEAKED CAP: Well?

CLARA: Next question. Please.

PEAKED CAP: Do you as a member of society contribute to that society's overall stability, cultural richness and general advancement?

CLARA: Oh, hmmm.

PEAKED CAP: Yes or no. All we need to do is check the appropriate box.

CLARA: Why don't I let you decide.

PEAKED CAP: Right. Next question. What, in ten words or less, is the purpose of your life?

CLARA: I was hoping you wouldn't ask that … just yet.

PEAKED CAP: Shall I leave it blank then?

CLARA: I think so. Yes.

PEAKED CAP: They won't like it.

CLARA: Any further questions?

PEAKED CAP: One more. This one's voluntary.

CLARA: Go ahead.

PEAKED CAP: Have you any advice for the teenage girls of today?

CLARA: Teenagers. Oh dear, I don't know all that many teenage girls anymore. There's my granddaughter, of course, and her friends, but they don't—

   (Music, loud rock, begins and interrupts conversation)

PEAKED CAP: I'll catch you next time.

   (CLARA and PEAKED CAP retreat to dressing room. All four women, in tune to rock music, pull winter coats, hats, scarves over basic costumes. They enter and sprawl on floor or platform with hands of cards. Music only gradually diminishes.)

WOMAN ONE [NORTH]: *(Shouting.)* I said, one diamond.

WOMAN TWO [EAST]: What?

WOMAN ONE: One diamond. Solitaire. One. Hey, woman, wanna turn that down.

WOMAN THREE [WEST]: I can't, you know, think without music, I just can't. I can't, you know?—concentrate kind-of-thing.

WOMAN FOUR [SOUTH]: How much longer before they open the box office?

WOMAN ONE: Three hours. *(They all groan.)*

WOMAN THREE: Okay. *(She reaches over and turns the radio off completely.)* You've got to say something, pass or else something above a diamond. Two something.

WOMAN TWO: How about ... two diamonds?

WOMAN FOUR: You can't say diamonds. That's ours. You can say anything else but.

WOMAN TWO: Clubs. Is that okay?

WOMAN ONE: As long as it's two. Or more.

WOMAN TWO: Hey! How do you remember all this stuff?

WOMAN ONE: Second nature, practically. I mean—it's like built into my chromosomes. I've been at it off and on for ten years.

WOMAN TWO: Huh? You must've learned in your high chair?

WOMAN ONE: Just about. I was ... *(Stops and thinks.)* seven years old, maybe ... maybe six.

WOMAN THREE: Come off it.

WOMAN ONE: No kidding. My mother? She belonged to this group? She still does—they call themselves—are you ready for this?—they call themselves The Edge of Night Gang. *(Said in booming opera tone.)*

WOMAN FOUR: The who?

WOMAN ONE: The Edge of Night, you know, like the old soap?

ALL: Oh yeah, sure, that thing. *(Etc.)*

WOMAN ONE: Well, they'd get together every Thursday night, only it used to be Wednesday afternoons back then, when none of them were working, just staying home doing the housewifey thing—

WOMAN TWO: Dusting the window sills—

WOMAN THREE: Wearing little aprons—

WOMAN ONE: Making lemon pies. All that stuff. So they got together Wednesday afternoons. Wednesdays were sacred, lemme tell you. They'd play for hours. Talking and getting socked on teeny little glasses of sherry.

WOMAN TWO: And pigging out on cashews.

WOMAN ONE: You've got it. Well, my mom used to get all dolled up, that's what she called it—these itty-bitty pincurls, and she'd sit under this hair dryer thing—

WOMAN FOUR: —with one of those bonnet things on her head? And the hose?

WOMAN ONE: Yeeaah!

WOMAN TWO: Far out.

WOMAN ONE: And she'd do her nails blood-red. She'd say, "Now have any of you seen my orange stick?" We didn't know what the hell she was talking about. She used to say it gave her a lift getting out like that.

WOMAN THREE: That's called a lift? Whew!

WOMAN ONE: My dad used to say, "Hey, how come you don't get dolled up for me, don't I rate? You'd think you were more in love with those gals than you are with me"—that's what he'd say, and, you know something—ha—it was probably true.

WOMAN TWO: In love—?

WOMAN ONE: They got off on each other, the four of them. My mom didn't know one single human when she first moved here—it was a company move, my dad's company,—and these three dames were the first people she met. This was back—hey, it must have been the fifties.

WOMAN TWO: Wow!

WOMAN ONE: You should have heard 'em talk. They never stopped. Only thing is, I can't remember what they used to talk about. They'd all talk at once, or at least that's how it sounded, and my dad had this standing joke. "Hey, who listens?" he'd ask her. Ha ha ha. Oh, she got so sick of him saying that every single week—"who listens?" It got on her nerves—she told me that after the divorce. Sort of broke the camel's back kind of thing?

WOMAN TWO: Yeah, well for my mom it was—

WOMAN ONE: Well, sometimes it would happen that there'd be an afternoon when one of The Edge of Nighters had to miss. Someone would get sick or go on a trip or maybe was having a baby—they were always having babies—once they were all preg-city at the same time. Mom said it was like they were sitting there with these watermelons on their laps. Well, this once, one of them called at the last minute. She couldn't come, some emergency or something, and so my mother said to me—I was home from school eating my lunch, a peanut butter and jam sandwich, probably, that's all I ate when I was a kid, I was a real brat—anyway, she said, "How'd you like to stay home this afternoon. I'll write your teacher a note, say you've got a sore throat."

Then she sat me down with a deck of cards and gave me a quickie lesson. Seven years old. Jeez. It was amazing, her sitting there pumping me full of all this stuff, all those rules, it was like she was someone else, someone, you know, nicer? Like we were two women, you know? Like girl friends or something. That's how I learned.

WOMAN THREE: I got it pumped into me too, but I mean like literally. My mother?—she used to take me with her when she played. It was hard to get baby-sitters in the daytime then and I was just a baby. She just stuck me in a corner in my little basket thingamajig, and if I got hungry and made a fuss, she'd whip out a boob right there at the table. Never missed a hand. A month old, two months old, and there I was, sucking up all those hearts and diamond tricks along with my mother's milk, God, I wonder what it tastes like.

WOMAN ONE: *(Reflecting.)* Vanilla ice cream—that's what I've heard, only melted.

WOMAN FOUR: Well, *(Long dramatic pause.)* you're not going to believe this but I swear to you it's the truth. My mother came home one night from the community club. She'd had this real heavy game. And it was the first time in her life she'd made a grand slam. Ever. She was high, she was in heaven, little birds singing kind of thing. She'd finally done it, know what I mean? It was a real rush.

WOMAN TWO: And?

WOMAN FOUR: That—that was the night I was conceived.

WOMAN TWO: I don't believe it.

WOMAN FOUR: It's the truth, I swear to God. I owe my life to a good spread of hearts.

WOMAN ONE: Hey, that's beautiful.

WOMAN FOUR: My dad probably didn't even know. They didn't talk about—you know—but my mother's friends all knew. Sometimes when I'd see them, they'd give me a little pat on the head and say, "Hi there, Grand Slam." God, I used to be so embarrassed. I'd just—it was crazy, I sort of loved it, though, if ya know what I mean.

WOMAN THREE: It's going to be different for us.

WOMAN FOUR: What? Making babies? Hey, I don't know about that.

WOMAN THREE: No. Not making babies.

WOMAN TWO: Well, what then?

WOMAN ONE: We're not going to need all that stuff. Those grand

slams, that other junk. Those afternoons. Setting your hair, doing your
nails. Dainties. Sherry. It'll be different. Like our bullshit isn't their
bullshit, you know?

WOMAN TWO: Yeah, but is it going to be better. Or worse?

WOMAN FOUR: Better. You better believe it, better.

WOMAN THREE: When I think of the exploitation.

WOMAN ONE: But, who ... who was exploiting them?

WOMAN THREE: What I mean is, they kind of like exploited themselves, know what I mean?

WOMAN TWO: All the same—I don't know, I've got this feeling—

WOMAN ONE: What?

WOMAN TWO: I was just going to say—at least it was better than—

WOMAN FOUR: At least they were kinda looking after each other, you
know?

WOMAN TWO: Let's start. Now. Let's not waste any time. We've
already wasted too much time.

WOMAN ONE: What do you mean? Start what?

WOMAN TWO: *(Desperately.)* Let's play. Let's ... *(She reaches for
radio and turns up the music.)* let's turn up the music. Come on, you
guys, let's *(She is shouting now.)* let's deal.

*(Lights fade; music fades. Lights come up on the elderly CLARA
seated at a table moving cards back and forth. She looks up and
addresses audience.)*

CLARA: That doctor—he was right about one thing, Ruthie didn't last
long. And after she went?—there was this one whole summer and fall
we didn't play. Tuesday nights would roll around and it would be like
any other night, but then Margot phoned me up one day and said she'd
run into Geraldine McMurtry who was a sort of cousin of hers, the
money side of the family, and Geraldine happened to say to Margot
how she liked a few hands now and then, nothing serious, and Margot
said to me, you know, maybe we should think of, you know, getting
started again, and so we did.

It gave me ... it gave me pause ... seeing Geraldine McMurtry sitting
here, in this chair. I found it ... upsetting. Well, she's very ... she's
got ... that is, compared to the rest of us, she's very ... comfortable.
That house! And those pearls of hers, they were real pearls. That first
night, she made Doris so nervous, she was biting her nails. It was her

manner of bidding, I think, not so much the pearls. Ruthie, well, Ruthie had always been a firm bidder, slow, but decided. But here was Geraldine. She sort of tore into her bids, just ripped in. Sometimes she'd open with, say, three hearts. Sometimes—whew, right into no-trump. Just lunged. Like she hadn't even taken time to count her points, only, in fact, she had. She was much, much sharper than she'd let on that day she ran into Margot, she'd fooled us in a way. And I don't know how it happened, but we all got kind of reckless too.

It changed us. Suddenly we were all playing these no-trump hands— but anyway, it was something to do on a Tuesday night. We got used to her, Geraldine. And I suppose … at first … she was getting used to us. She hated being dummy, she'd tap her fingernails on the edge of the table or else pull out her knitting … with a kind of jerk … but she relaxed after a bit. And she could make us laugh, Margot especially, it was something to see, Margot going off in, in gales.

It was a funny thing about Margot. In all those years—it was forty-three years in all, we were young women when we started out, just newly married, all of us—in all that time Margot's husband, Ronald—Ronald thought she spent her each and every Tuesday night doing knitting for the Martha Circle. *(Long pause.)* He was a Baptist, Ronald, all his life. No drinking, no dancing, no this, no that. So we had this code word. I'd call up Margot and say, "Martha Circle's meeting at Doris's next Tuesday," or, if something came up, "Martha Circle's canceled this week." Oh, she hated that, when we had to cancel for some reason or other. Oh my. The Martha Circle.

We used to say to her, tell him, face up to him. Own up to it. But the thing was, she left it too late. *(As she talks she moves cards about.)* It's one thing to face up to a young husband and get your way. A young girl can do pretty well anything she wants. It's something else to sneak around for forty-three years, making up lies and excuses. *(Holds up a card.)* The devil's eyelids, that's what Ronald called these—he'd been brought up in a strict household. Well, we said to Margot, explain to him there's just as much skill as chance involved, maybe more, but she just shook her head.

I think it made her ashamed, even though we made a joke about it. "Who's going to cut the devil's eyelids?" we'd say, that sort of thing. You'd think we'd get sick from laughing, oh, we'd howl.

(Picks up cards and starts again.)

After Margot was … gone, about a year after, and Ronald asked me, asked me if I would do him the honour, the honour of being his wife, well, I said I had to think about that a bit, you'll have to give me some time, I said. He said, here we are, Clara, the two of us, we've known each other for donkey's years, and now we're each of us left on our lonesome, your Arthur gone to his reward, and my poor Margot. You and I, we could be company for each other. And I said to Ronald, yes, that's true enough, but I needed time to think about it.

Well, I screwed up my nerve and went and asked Doris, what did she think. Luckily I caught her on one of her good days. I said, did she think Margot would have had any objection if Ronald and I ... and she said, Doris said, on the contrary, just the opposite, that Margot would have taken it as a compliment. Another thing Doris said was Ronald Hetherling's a good-hearted man and he's got ... the loveliest head of hair you've ever seen on someone that age.

So I said to Ronald, yes, but on one condition, that on Tuesday nights I was ... occupied ... with my Martha Circle. He gave me a look. And cleared his throat. On Tuesday nights, he told me, he himself attends his adult bible class. In the church basement, it's been going on for years and years, and they're still in the prophets. He goes out every Tuesday night, he stressed that particular point, from seven to ten o'clock, and he wanted me to go on doing what I'd always been doing because it meant a great deal to me, he knew that.

(She gathers up cards, stacks them slowly; the clock chimes; when it reaches ten strokes, she puts cards in her pocket. Clock strikes fourteen times. Lights fade almost completely, then come up brilliantly. She sits up straight, suddenly younger, WOMAN ONE [WEST].

Three other women enter briskly, joining WOMAN ONE and taking their places at card table. They are all talking at once as the cards are rapidly dealt out and hands taken up and arranged.)

WOMAN ONE: *(Simultaneously.)*—so the wind starting blowing like crazy—

WOMAN TWO [SOUTH]: *(Simultaneously.)*—dead tired, but the floors to do—

WOMAN THREE [EAST]: *(Simultaneously.)*—half a pound of sugar, not half a cup—

WOMAN FOUR [NORTH]: *(Simultaneously.)*—never could add two and two—

(Pause.)

WOMAN ONE: *(Simultaneously.)*—Victoria Day picnic after all—

WOMAN TWO: *(Simultaneously.)*—swallowing an upholstery tack and—

WOMAN THREE: *(Simultaneously.)*—specialized in steam fitting which I thought—

WOMAN FOUR: *(Simultaneously.)*—two yards of grosgrain ribbon around the border—

(Pause.)

WOMAN ONE: *(Simultaneously.)*—the most terrible headache and his ears too—

WOMAN TWO: *(Simultaneously.)*—an out and out lie, but what did I know?

WOMAN THREE: *(Simultaneously.)*—a sight for sore eyes, I told her, but she said—

WOMAN FOUR: *(Simultaneously.)*—deaf as a stone after the age of sixty-five—

(Pause.)

WOMAN ONE: Two clubs.

WOMAN TWO: Pass.

WOMAN THREE: Two spades?

WOMAN FOUR: —she said interrogatively. Pass.

WOMAN ONE: Three spades.

WOMAN TWO: —she said emphatically. Pass.

WOMAN THREE: Pass.

WOMAN FOUR: Pass.

WOMAN ONE: Dummy again. Which reminds me—

(Here she raises her hands in the air and switches into a rapid-fire recitative style.)

My grandson Trevor, you remember Trevor, oh that boy, well he scored a zero on his algebra test and not only that he was rude to the teacher who sent him down to the principal's office where they made him sit for two hours and twenty minutes twiddling his thumbs and scared to death the whole time of getting expelled—now do you think that's fair—I was so burned up I just had to tell you.

WOMAN TWO: Tell away! Better to get it off your chest.

WOMAN THREE: Absolutely.

WOMAN FOUR: Why do you think we're sitting at this table—

WOMAN THREE: *(Singing.)* That's what we're here for—

WOMAN TWO: *(Singing.)* don't ya know.

ALL: *(Singing; drumming on table.)* That's what we're here for, don't ya know.

WOMAN TWO: *(Recitative.)* Just between you and me and the lamp-post I can't bear to think that I am now the wife of a grandfather—with whom if the truth were known I sometimes have vicious quarrels about foolish things like for instance putting too much detergent in the dishwater and not rinsing prop-er-ly and then one of us or both of us starts in calling the other one an ungrateful hard-hearted insensitive so-and-so—

WOMAN ONE: Just lay it on us. Just let it go.

ALL: *(Singing; drumming table.)* That's what we're here for don't ya know.

WOMAN THREE: *(Recitative.)* I feel I can't keep this to myself for one minute longer—I am so bloody sick and tired of making things for bazaars—hideous things—things made out of orange nylon—things nobody in God's creation wants or needs or appre-ciates—sure I know it's not worth making a fuss about, so tell me, why do I want to climb up on a soapbox and scream and rage and tell the whole wide world where to gooooo.

ALL: *(Singing; drumming table.)* Hey, tell us about it, tell us about it,
That's what we're here for, that's what we're here for—
Sitting at this table, sitting at this table, sitting here, sitting here—
Don't ya know.

WOMAN FOUR: *(Recitative.)* So she turned around and said to me in this loud snarky voice, "This is the express line, madam—can't you see this is the express line—only nine items allowed, madam, and you have at least twelve in your basket, madam—that's the rule, nine items," and I said, "Oh I'm so sorry, I guess I was thinking of something else"—feeling like a complete and utter fool—and for days I've been walking around feeling lower than low—

ALL: *(Singing; drumming table.)* Let it out, just let it out,
That's what we're here for
Sitting at this table, sitting at this table,
Don't ya know.

WOMAN ONE: *(Recitative or speaking.)* Listen, my friends, something's wrong with me, something's terribly wrong—lately I keep forgetting things—I keep losing things, my purse, my slippers, my famous recipe for mango chutney, I've become one of those women, you know the type, who's always rummaging in her purse, rummage, rummage, and—this is the worst part—most of the time I can't remember what the hell I'm rummaging for—oh, my God, sometimes I sit in the dark and cry for no good reason—I mean, tell me, honestly, do you think it's just hormones or what—?

WOMAN TWO: *(Recitative, quietly.)* My husband got this statuette for working for the same company for forty-five years and I wanted him to put it on the mantle—this is something to be proud of, I said, but do you know what he did—he put it in a green garbage bag and put a twist tie around it—he actually went and took the darn thing to the dump.

WOMAN FOUR: *(Recitative.)* I'll never understand men, I'll never understand my in-laws, I'll never understand my children, my grandchildren, my grade three teacher and as for that snarky woman in Safeway—I can't stop thinking how mad I am at, at, at—

WOMAN ONE: *(Speaking.)* Never mind. Just let it out.

WOMAN TWO: *(Speaking.)* Our ears are open.

WOMAN THREE: *(Speaking.)* You'll feel better.

WOMAN ONE: A helluva lot better.

WOMAN TWO: You know what they say about bottling things up.

WOMAN THREE: Just let it go.

WOMAN ONE: *(Recitative.)* I hate to sound like I'm complaining but I'm so fed up with colouring my hair, tinting my hair, dying my goddamn hair, I mean my mother had gray hair, why can't I have gray hair, gray hair done up in a teensy-weensy itsy-bitsy bun, do you understand what I'm saying, a lit-tle gray bun, here!—with a rubber band around it, here!—

WOMAN TWO: *(Speaking.)* Really?

WOMAN THREE: *(Recitative.)* If that's what you want—

WOMAN ONE: *(Screams.)* That's what I want.

WOMAN THREE: Go for it, as my grandson would say.

WOMAN FOUR: *(Recitative.)* Sometimes—sometimes I feel invisible. It started not long after my fiftieth birthday—I could feel people looking right past me, looking for someone more attractive, looking for someone more interesting to talk to—it's like I'm not here anymore—am I crazy or what?

WOMAN TWO: *(Recitative.)* I know juuuust what you meeeean—

WOMAN ONE: *(Recitative.)* The saaaame thing happens to meeee—

WOMAN THREE: *(Recitative.)*—and to meeeeeee *(Holds high note as long as possible.)*

WOMAN ONE: —and to meeee.

ALL: —meeeeee.

WOMAN TWO: What can we do, what can we do?

WOMAN THREE: *(Speaking, struck by idea.)* Hey, if we're invisible, doesn't that mean we can do anything we want? Rude things. Appalling things. Hideous things.

WOMAN ONE: *(Recitative.)* Let it out, just let it out, let it goooo.

(Pause. They all sing.)

ALL: That's what we're here for, that's what we're here for,
Sitting round the table, sitting round the table,
That's what we're here for,
Don't ya know.

(Women retire to dressing room, softly carrying on with chorus. Music gradually fades. Light comes up on four women seated around a card table. They are wearing hats of a vaguely fifties fashion. Their postures and voices betray their nervousness. One of them has just dropped a sherry glass on the floor and broken it.)

WOMAN ONE [NORTH]: Oh! Oh, I'm so sorry, I don't know how I—

WOMAN TWO [WEST]: Please. It's nothing.

(Pats WOMAN ONE's hand comfortingly and starts to pick pieces off floor. All four women dive to floor to help with clean up.)

WOMAN ONE: Such a beautiful crystal glass. I don't know how I could have been so—*(To herself.)* Damn, now I've done it. Oh, damn, damn, damn, damn. At least the damn thing was empty.

WOMAN TWO: Please, please don't give it another thought. Really, it isn't at all valuable. *(To herself.)* If she only knew. Crystal, ha! Thirty-nine cents at Woolworths.

WOMAN THREE [SOUTH]: Careful, don't cut yourself. *(To herself.)* Bad enough I overbid on that last hand. Brian warned me about overbidding.

(Women rise and take their places again.)

WOMAN TWO: *(To WOMAN ONE.)* I'll just get you another glass of sherry. *(To herself.)* I can't stand it, the way she's looking at me. Oh, no, she's going to cry. I cannot stand this.

WOMAN ONE: Oh, no, thank you, I've had enough, thank you just the same. *(To herself.)* Enough, ha. I'm drunk. I am drunk. Hee hee. I'm high as a kite, I'm flying.

WOMAN FOUR [EAST]: *(Anxious to change subject.)* Well. Shall I deal then? *(To herself.)* I wish she'd offer *me* another sherry. Not that I need it. Whew.

WOMAN THREE: I'm not sure, but I think, if I'm not mistaken, I think it's ... maybe ... my ... deal? *(To herself.)* I wonder if I sound pushy, overbearing. But it really is my deal. At least I think it is.

WOMAN FOUR: Oh, of course, how stupid of me. *(To herself, Southern accent.)* Ah'm just sooo stew-pid. Pu-leese! The stupid part was saying I'd come here today. I'm going to kill Jonathan when I get home. Roping me into this!

WOMAN THREE: *(Dealing.)* Oh, sorry, misdeal. I'll start over. *(To herself.)* What's the matter with me. My hands are ... they're sweating. This is real sweat. Wet sweat. And my underarms, I wonder if I smell. This is like being a teenager again. Worse. Why did I let myself in for this?

WOMAN ONE: About that sherry glass, I really would like to pay for it. I'd feel better.

WOMAN TWO: *(To herself.)* Can't she just forget it. *(Out loud.)* Honestly, I wouldn't dream of letting you.

WOMAN ONE: *(To herself.)* I don't know why she's serving sherry anyway. Especially sweet sherry. I could puke. My mother always used to serve tea. Orange pekoe. And date squares.

WOMAN TWO: *(To herself.)* I shouldn't have listened to Thurston. I knew I should have stuck with tea or coffee. I think—I think she's a little ... drunk.

WOMAN THREE: I'm going to say ... one heart. *(To herself.)* Well, just say it then, why don't ya. One little buttery heart.

WOMAN TWO: *(To herself.)* I wish I was drunk. Veddy, veddy drunk.

WOMAN THREE: Ahem. *(Repeating.)* One heart? *(To herself.)* Pretty timid bid, but I don't dare overbid again. The way she glared at me. At least I think she was glaring. How'm I supposed to know without my glasses on? Why didn't I wear them. Who cares. *She's* got glasses on. Gawd, are they hideous, too.

WOMAN TWO: Pass. *(To herself.)* I wonder if they noticed the fruit-cake was underdone. They did eat it. They chewed. And they swallowed, but they swallowed in a kind of thick, cakey way. *(Whimpers.)* Maybe—maybe that's why they drank so much sherry.

WOMAN ONE: Two hearts. *(To herself.)* Do it for me, he said. It's important, meeting the other company wives. What the hell does he know about company wives.

WOMAN FOUR: Pass. *(To herself.)* Coward. And with twelve points in my hand! I wonder if anyone'll notice.

WOMAN THREE. Pass. *(To herself.)* I should go to three, but I'd better not chance it. Brian's always saying how reckless I get. We could actually have a little slam here … no, better not.

WOMAN FOUR: *(To herself.)* I'm the only one here whose purse and shoes don't match.

WOMAN ONE: *(To herself.)* I've got to forget that damn broken glass.

WOMAN TWO: *(To herself.)* I don't care what Thurston says, I'm not cut out to be the boss's wife. Charming, sweet, thoughtful. Argggh.

WOMAN THREE: *(To herself.)* The next time she invites us, I'm going to say I'm sick. I'll say something like, like I've got a migraine. Or I'm waiting for a long distance call from … my sister or something. How's she going to know I don't have a sister.

WOMAN ONE: *(To herself.)* And Mother actually enjoyed this. But that was different.

WOMAN THREE: *(To herself.)* My nail polish. Chipped. And I just did them before I came. Brian always says—

WOMAN ONE: *(To herself.)* I'll send her a little hasty note, tell her how *frightfully* sorry I am about her dumb, stupid, idiotic, unspeakable, precious two-bit sherry glass—

WOMAN TWO: *(To herself.)* I should have served chocolate chip cookies. Why do I always listen to Thurston. What does he know anyway? Next time I'll serve—if there is a next time. If only they'd go home—

WOMAN THREE: *(To herself.)* I wish I was home. It's four o'clock. I could be flaked out on the couch, my feet up, watching The Edge of Night. I wonder if Sarah's going to tell Steve about the baby's real father today.

WOMAN FOUR: God, I'm wrecking the cards, clenching them like this. *(To herself.)* I wish this was over.

WOMAN ONE: *(To herself.)* I wish I was dead.

WOMAN TWO: You made it. Two hearts.

WOMAN FOUR: Well played.

WOMAN THREE: I can't believe it, what luck.

WOMAN ONE: *(To herself.)* When I think Mother did this every Tuesday night for ... forty years, the four of them. Doris Veal, Auntie Doris, she was a bit scary, and Clara Wesley and Margot Hetherling. *(Out loud.)* When I think of it, my mother used to play every Tuesday night, for forty years.

WOMAN TWO: Really! That's ... *(Hunts for word.)* marvelous.

WOMAN THREE: My mother too. Only it was Saturdays. They'd start off with a potluck lunch, macaroni and tuna things, or something creamed on patty shells, and then—

WOMAN FOUR: With our family it was the back porch. In the summer time. We'd play until it got dark. Men against the women. My uncles, my grandfather, cousins. There'd be mosquitoes buzzing like mad in front of our faces, but we'd keep—

WOMAN ONE: I used to lie in bed and listen to them downstairs in the living room. I could smell their cigarette smoke drifting up the—of course they all smoked like chimneys—

WOMAN TWO: Well, people did then.

WOMAN ONE: *(To herself.)* God, I could use a fag right now. Doesn't this woman own any ashtrays?

WOMAN THREE: *(Desperately.)* Good heavens, I just noticed the time, I hate to break this up, but I've got to get on my way. *(To herself.)* Oi, oi, now that was pretty smooth!

WOMAN FOUR: Me too. Jonathan likes me to be there when he comes in the door. He likes dinner waiting, likes to walk in and smell dinner cooking, he says it's the best part of his—*(To herself.)* My God, I'm babbling, stop it, stop it.

WOMAN TWO: I'll just get your coats.

WOMAN ONE: *(Rising.)* My mother was only fifty-nine when she died. Cancer. Of the uterus. The rest of them, they went on for years. One of them, Clara Wesley, she phoned me specially and asked me if I minded that they went on, as if I'd mind. As if I as the daughter would be offended that my mother's friends were carrying on. Isn't that amazing? They were like these strange extra aunts, coming in through the door, winter nights in their heavy coats, summer time in cotton dresses, all the time I was growing up.

WOMAN FOUR: My mother died of cancer too. It was all through her.

WOMAN THREE: My mother still plays, every Saturday. There were eight of them back in the old days. Now they're down to four. I don't know what they'll do when—

WOMAN ONE: When my mother died, afterwards, I was going through her things, sorting through her gloves and her purses, all those things, and her hats—she loved hats. Oh, not little pie plate things like we wear today. Big hats. They meant something. Well, I was emptying out one of her dresser drawers and what should I come across but a bunch of old card-party tallies. Oh, I can't tell you, they were lovely. *(Her voice breaks.)*

WOMAN FOUR: Here. *(Hands tissue.)*

WOMAN ONE: They had these ... little silk tassels on them.

WOMAN TWO: You mustn't upset yourself.

WOMAN ONE: *(Dry eyed now.)* They were always laughing. Laughing to beat the band, as they would have said. One of them, Doris, I think she used to tell—

WOMAN FOUR: What?

WOMAN ONE: Well ... stories. Maybe a tiny bit off-colour. I couldn't hear very well, but that's what it sounded like, from the way they were laughing. I couldn't believe it was my mother. I never heard her really laugh except on those Tuesday nights. They were so ... gay.

WOMAN TWO: My mother, she didn't have much chance for a good time ... we were out on this god-forsaken farm, eight of us kids—

WOMAN FOUR: Well, thank you so much. It's been—

WOMAN ONE: Their voices would come up through the hot air register. I tried to listen, but I couldn't make out exactly—

WOMAN THREE: A very pleasant afternoon. Thank you for asking me. I appreciate—

WOMAN TWO: Maybe we could do it again. I don't actually know all that many people here—

WOMAN FOUR: I don't know a soul.

WOMAN THREE: Well, I'm not sure, I'm pretty busy, and my sister might be—

WOMAN ONE: Maybe you'd like to come to my place next time.

WOMAN TWO: Well—

WOMAN ONE: Only thing, we haven't got around to getting a card table yet, and the dining room table's too big, but maybe, there's always the kitchen table—

WOMAN FOUR: That's no problem, the kitchen table.

WOMAN ONE: And another thing, we're having our floors sanded and it's pretty dusty. Maybe you could come in something—

WOMAN FOUR: Casual?

WOMAN TWO: We could wear ... *(As though struck with inspiration.)* sports clothes.

WOMAN FOUR: Should we set a date?

WOMAN THREE: If we could make it a little earlier? I always watch, well ... The Edge of Night.

WOMAN TWO: Oh, so do I.

WOMAN FOUR: Me too. As a matter of fact, I was just wondering, if Sarah and Steve were going to—

WOMAN ONE: How about next week, next Wednesday. A few hands, and then we'll put the TV on. We can, you know, just see how it goes.

(Lights dim; give way to tape of women talking and laughing. Three women exit to dressing room, leaving CLARA behind. Light softens. Clarinet music. FLOWERY HAT [SOUTH], wearing a large flowery hat, mounts bicycle, riding to centre stage, ringing bicycle bell importantly.)

FLOWERY HAT: You must be Clara. Clara Wesley.

CLARA: *(Rummaging in her purse.)* Actually, it's Clara Hetherling now. Now what did I do with those keys of mine?

FLOWERY HAT: Of course. Mrs. Hetherling. That's the name I have on this form.

CLARA: There they are, my keys. I knew they were there. Now, if I can just put my hands on my specs ...

FLOWERY HAT: I see you're still rushing around, getting ready to go out, getting ready for an evening with your friends. I see you've become the kind of person who's always rummaging in her purse, I see you're a little older.

CLARA: Older?—well, yes, I suppose. We all get older, don't we. Now if you'll excuse me I really must—I can't see a thing without my specs.

FLOWERY HAT: I see you're still going on with your life, Clara. That is, I see your life is going on with you.

CLARA: Well, I suppose you could say—

FLOWERY HAT: I find it strange, don't you, the way a human life drains down toward one thing, just one little revealing thing.

CLARA: What thing? What do you mean, thing? Now I really must concentrate—where did I put those—

FLOWERY HAT: This game you play, this Tuesday night game the four of you *hurl* yourselves into—

CLARA: *(Finding specs.)* Here they are, thank the Lord. *(Rushing away.)*

FLOWERY HAT: *(Calling after her.)* This game of yours. Can you tell me about this game.

CLARA: *(Turning impatiently but politely.)* I'm terribly late.

FLOWERY HAT: This game.

CLARA: Oh, for heaven's sake. *(Laughs.)* For heaven's sakes. *(Quietly, puzzled herself.)* It isn't—it isn't just a *game*, you know.

(Music. Lights fade. End of Act One.)

Act Two

(Song: to be sung in lobby during last three or four minutes of intermission or on stage as opening of Act Two. Four women wearing beads and long white gloves take their places at card table. Song is operetta style, sung with Gilbert and Sullivan lightness.)

ALL: It's not a sin—no it's not a sin—
  It's not a sin, sin, sin, sin, sin,
  To want to win, win, win, win,
  Competit-ion is not necessar-ily
  a sin.

  It's only nat-ural, it's o-nly fair,
  To come up breathing—na-tural com-pet-i-tive air.
  To want to win, win, win, win,
  Is not a sin, no, no, it's not a sin.
  So let's be-ginnnnn.

  (Piano repeat.)

SOUTH: A very fine hand
  Is all I ask, it's all I ask,
  A decent hand is what I require
  To make the e-vening catch fire.

ALL: A very fine hand
  Is all she asks, is all she asks,
  A decent hand is what she requires
  To make the e-vening catch fire.
  It's not a sin—you know, you know—to want to win.

EAST and WEST: A run of spades will bring us luck,
   Will bring us luck, will bring us luck,
   With King and Queen—and Ace and Jack—
   It's all we need—a little luck.

ALL: A King and Queen and Ace and Jack
   It's all they need, a little luck.
   A little luck, a little luck,
   Or a little more than a little luck,
   A little more than a little luck.
   It's not a sin—you know—to want to win,
   It's not a sin, no, no, it's not a sin.
   So let's be-gin.

SOUTH and NORTH: It's not a crime to take your time,
   No, it's not a crime to take your time,
   Their reason's sound, they're off the ground,
   They'll bring the e-vening around.

ALL: We'll bring the e-vening around,
   Oh, we'll bring the e-vening around.
   It's not a sinnnn
   To want to winnnn
   So breast your cards, my friends,
   And we'll begin.

NORTH: We'll counter with—our sturdy hearts,
   Our mighty hearts, our bleeding hearts,
   With length and strength in bloody hearts
   We'll bring a crushing bid to start.

ALL: Ooooo-oooo-oooo
   Trump, trump, trump, trump,
   Trump, trump, trump, trump.
   Taking in those gorgeous trumps,
   It's not a sin, to want to win.
   We're on our way—to victory.
   Trump, trump, trump, trump.

EAST and WEST: One, two three, four five six, seven,
   Trump, trump, trump, trump,
   Trump, trump, trump, trump.

   (Carry on beat through next chorus.)

SOUTH and NORTH: We'll open with a lead to trump.

EAST and WEST: We won't be stumped by a lead to trump.

SOUTH: We'll open low, then third hand high
  And that will be our strat-ta-gy.

ALL: They'll open with a lead to trump,
  They'll thump them hard with a lead to trump,
  They'll open low low low,
  Then third hand high high high,
  That is to be—their strat-ta-gy.

SOUTH and NORTH: Trump, trump, trump, trump,
  Trump, trump, trump, trump.

EAST and WEST: And now the tricks come rolling in,
  Come rolling in, come rolling in,
  We'll make our bid or go down low,
  This is the way—the game will go.

SOUTH and NORTH: We must confess—a bold finesse,
  We must confess—yes, yes, yes, yes,
  A bold finesse.
  It's not a sin—you know, to want to win.

ALL: Club and diamond, hearts and spades,
  And tricks and trumps—and masquerades—
  With luck and cun-ning, we'll raid and trade—
  This isn't—you know—the ladies aid.

No, no, no, no, it's not a sin
To want to win.

  (All rise from table, repeat.)

Club and diamond, hearts and spades
And tricks and trumps—and masquerades—
With luck and cun-ning, we'll raid and trade—
This isn't—you know—the ladies aid.

No, no, no, no, it's not a sin
To want to win
So let's begin.

  (Lights come up on card table. The women are The Edge of Night foursome, a few years older.)

WOMAN TWO [WEST]: And we were so close to making it! If we'd just made that club trick, it would have been ours.

WOMAN FOUR [EAST]: Oh, God, I'm sorry.

WOMAN ONE [NORTH]: Hey, hey, hey, since when did we start apologizing.

WOMAN FOUR: My second boob this afternoon. What's the matter with me?

WOMAN TWO: Anyone can have a bad day.

WOMAN THREE [SOUTH]: Don't I know it. Remember last week. My God, I bombed with my diamonds. Twenty-one points and I took a royal nose dive. Sheesh.

WOMAN FOUR: *(Shuffles cards, which suddenly slide out of her hands.)* Oh, no, look what I did now.

WOMAN ONE: Maybe we should quit. There's not really enough time for another game.

WOMAN THREE: We could have a quickie—

WOMAN TWO: Okay, one more hand.

WOMAN FOUR: *(Taking a deep breath.)* Listen, maybe we'd better ... not. I've got ... something to say. An announcement, sort of. I've been putting it off and putting it off, oh look, but maybe I should just say it fast and get it over with.

WOMAN ONE: What gives? You sound ... serious.

WOMAN FOUR: I am ... serious.

WOMAN THREE: Go on.

WOMAN FOUR: I don't know how to tell you this. All of you. I meant to tell you right away, when we first got here this afternoon, but—

WOMAN TWO: You can't—you can't be—

WOMAN THREE: Not at your—I mean, you had your tubes—

WOMAN FOUR: No, no, no, it's, well, oh, this is harder than I thought—

WOMAN TWO: You haven't got a brain tumor.

WOMAN ONE: A brain tumor! What made you think of a brain tumor?

WOMAN TWO: I dunno, I guess I was thinking of that time way back when Steve on The Edge of Night—

WOMAN FOUR: It's nothing like that. It's something ... completely different. It's just that—I've—

WOMAN ONE: Come on, take it easy. You're going to feel a whole lot better once you've got whatever it is off your—

WOMAN FOUR: It's just that I've, well, I've come to ... a decision.

WOMAN TWO: I can't stand this.

WOMAN FOUR: It was a very, very tough decision to make, for, for all kinds of reasons.

WOMAN ONE: Oh, my God, no. I knew it. My sixth sense. You're leaving—

WOMAN THREE: You're leaving Jonathan.

WOMAN FOUR: I, actually I—

WOMAN TWO: I saw this coming. I saw it coming for a looooonng time. I never said anything, but I did see—

WOMAN ONE: Listen, listen, you've got to get this in proportion. Okay, so it's a major decision but it's not the end of the world. And, who knows, it just might be the best decision you've ever made. You may just—

WOMAN FOUR: I—

WOMAN TWO: You've put up with a lot.

WOMAN THREE: That's for sure.

WOMAN ONE: We know Jonathan hasn't exactly been—

WOMAN FOUR: Look, I'm—

WOMAN ONE: You're going to be just fine. You'll come through this. And we'll support you—

WOMAN THREE: —every inch of the way.

WOMAN TWO: I just wish I had the courage. I look at Thurston and I think—is this the same man I married. Sometimes he's such a, such a—

WOMAN ONE: Jerk. Even Brian says—

WOMAN THREE: Precisely. And Jerry says exactly the—

WOMAN FOUR: Actually—

WOMAN TWO: I was serving this salad? Oooooo! A new recipe—you take cracked wheat, olive oil, green onions, and just before serving you add a handful of currants.

WOMAN THREE: Currants? You mean like raisins?

WOMAN TWO: It's supposed to be Mediterranean.

WOMAN ONE: Sounds really ... interesting.

WOMAN TWO: Well, I was right in the middle of serving it, there were eight of us at the table—

WOMAN ONE: Clients, I suppose. Trust Thurston.

WOMAN TWO: As a matter of fact, it was my sister-in-law Edna and her family. We were eating this salad, and do you know what Thurston said?

WOMAN THREE: I can't stand it. What?

WOMAN TWO: He said, "What exactly are these rabbit droppings doing in the salad?" He was just ... being ... funny, his little joke, ha ha ha, but something, something awful came over me. Like my scalp was freezing. And burning at the same time. Rabbit droppings. Dodo in my Mediterranean salad. I wanted to reach across the table and ... tear his ears off.

WOMAN FOUR: Never mind his ears, you should've gone for his—

WOMAN ONE: You don't have to sit there and take what Thurston dishes out—

WOMAN THREE: You know something, I've got a pretty good idea what Jerry would do if he saw currants in one of my salads. He wouldn't say anything, but he'd roll his eyes. Oh, boy, that gets to me, when he rolls his—

WOMAN FOUR: Look, I want to—

WOMAN THREE: In eleven years, I don't think there's been one day when he hasn't ... rolled his—

WOMAN ONE: *(Sympathetically.)* Jesus, that's—

WOMAN THREE: I'll do something or I'll say something, some little thing, and up go his—Zoom. They go right *through* me, right ... through my heart.

WOMAN TWO: And you put up with that?

WOMAN THREE: I've thought seriously about leaving him. But what am I supposed to tell people, that I'm leaving my husband because he rolls—?

WOMAN TWO: Listen, you don't have to explain anything to anybody. You just have to get up and go.

WOMAN ONE: Or tell him to go. That's what I'd say. Out. Here's the door, there's the door knob—out! Only before he left I'd show him the Eaton's bill. Get a gander at this, I'd say. A hundred and fifty dollars. A hundred and fifty smackers paid out to Eaton's. A cosmetic item. Perfume. French, no less. Explain that if you don't mind.

WOMAN THREE: What are you talking about? What Eaton's bill? What perfume?

WOMAN ONE: What perfume—that's what I wanted to know. There it was on February's statement, a hundred and fifty dollar charge. Does he honestly think I'm not going to phone the store and ask what's what.

WOMAN TWO: I had no idea he was the type to—

WOMAN ONE: And believe me ... believe me, it isn't ... the first time.

WOMAN TWO: Why on earth have you stayed with him?

WOMAN ONE: I've thought about it a lot. Especially lately. I mean, the kids are old enough to understand. He could get an apartment downtown, see them on weekends, not that he takes all that much interest in them anyway. The last time he—

WOMAN THREE: And you'd keep the house?

WOMAN ONE: I could rent out the basement to a couple of university students. The money would help. And, well, to tell you the out and out truth, I wouldn't mind the company. Someone to, you know, chew over the day with, what did you do? what did *you* do? that kind of thing.

WOMAN TWO: Why not? We all need—

WOMAN THREE: You might be lonely. You know, at night.

WOMAN TWO: I don't know about that. When Thurston's away on business trips I just love it. You know what I do? I eat peanuts. I just sit in front of the TV and eat peanuts and no one ever says—hey, what about those saddlebags of yours.

WOMAN ONE: Talk about the pot calling the kettle—

WOMAN TWO: Exactly.

WOMAN THREE: I think, if I was on my own that is, I think I'd probably become a vegetarian, Jerry hates salad but I could eat it three times a day, I could really get into the whole holistic thing—

WOMAN FOUR: Well, I—

WOMAN ONE: You've got to be careful about your lawyer. Really check it out, get hold of someone who's got a few progressive ideas about—

WOMAN TWO: As a matter of fact I have the name of an excellent—

WOMAN THREE: The best thing to do, once you've made the decision, I mean, is go to a completely different city. If Jerry ever—

WOMAN TWO: A clean break. Absolutely right.

WOMAN THREE: Now, I've always—well, the fact is—I've always loved Montreal.

WOMAN ONE: Your French is terrific—

WOMAN THREE: Not exactly terrific, but I could brush up—

WOMAN TWO: I've got a line on a marvelous French course that's being offered—remind me to drop this brochure off for you.

WOMAN THREE: Why thanks, I'd appreciate that.

WOMAN ONE: I've said to him, one more time and it's over.

WOMAN TWO: I think I'd probably get myself a little puppy for company. Or maybe a *big* dog. Springer spaniels are nice. I've always wanted one. Thurston hates dogs but—

WOMAN THREE: Jerry too, can't abide them.

WOMAN TWO: —But if … if I was on my own, if Thurston wasn't … around, well, a dog can be excellent company. Better than—

WOMAN ONE: I think you should definitely go for a dog.

WOMAN THREE: I'd redo the living room. If I was on my own. Go in for a, you know, a Mediterranean look.

WOMAN ONE: What I'd do is sell the piano. Definitely.

WOMAN TWO: I'd put a skylight in the bathroom. Right away. Thurston says they're useless in this climate but—

WOMAN THREE: Jerry says they're a drain on the heating system.

WOMAN TWO: But they do let in a lot of light. And if it was up to me—

WOMAN THREE: If Thurston wasn't there—

WOMAN ONE: Why not. You need a change now and then. I've only hung on to that dumb piano because it belongs to *his* side of the family. Left on my own I'd—

WOMAN TWO: No one would blame you for a minute.

WOMAN FOUR: I—I—

WOMAN ONE: I just, just … *(Close to tears.)* I just want to get out while I still have a shred of dignity left.

WOMAN THREE: Listen, we'll stand by you. You know that, don't you.

WOMAN TWO: The problem is—

WOMAN ONE: The problem is, well, doing it.

WOMAN THREE: What do you mean?

WOMAN TWO: I know what you mean.

WOMAN ONE: Sometimes I think, I think it takes more courage than I've got.

WOMAN TWO: Me too. I say, hey, I'm comfortable enough. In some ways. Sometimes I'm even—

WOMAN THREE: Once I wrote him a note. A good-bye, this-thing-is-over note. I left it on the fridge.

WOMAN TWO: Really? You did?

WOMAN THREE: I thought, he'll sneak down in the middle of the night and make one of his revolting mayo and raspberry jam sandwich combos and he'll see it.

WOMAN ONE: And what did he say?

WOMAN THREE: I tore it up at the last minute. I just didn't have ... the courage.

WOMAN ONE: *(To WOMAN FOUR.)* That's why, that's why I admire you for the decision you've taken. It takes real guts.

WOMAN TWO: And then you've got to bear in mind that Jonathan's going to recover in time and you'll heal too.

WOMAN THREE: You'll look back and think that leaving Jonathan was the best decision you've ever made.

WOMAN FOUR: But I'm not.

WOMAN ONE: Not what?

WOMAN FOUR: Not leaving Jonathan.

WOMAN TWO: You're not—?

WOMAN ONE: You're not leaving Jonathan?

WOMAN FOUR: I'm getting a job.

WOMAN THREE: A job.

WOMAN FOUR: It's in personnel. It's perfect for me, tailor made, you might say.

WOMAN THREE: But Jonathan—?

WOMAN FOUR: Well, it was Jonathan actually who happened to hear about this job. He's been encouraging me to go back to work for years. But it's been a god-awful decision. It means—well, it means I have to give up ... our Wednesday afternoons.

WOMAN ONE: Jesus Christ.

WOMAN TWO: My God.

WOMAN THREE: I can't believe it. A job!

WOMAN TWO: Actually ... I was thinking ... myself, of maybe, looking around for a ... something part-time maybe ...

(They all begin talking at once.)

WOMAN FOUR: Personnel can be the key in an up and coming firm—

WOMAN ONE: I'd need to brush up on my skills, do some kind of refresher course—

WOMAN TWO: I'd have to think seriously about how I'd handle myself in an interview and—

WOMAN THREE: I've had this gnawing feeling, you know, a kind of empty feeling, and maybe what I should do is–

WOMAN FOUR: Of course I'll have to modify my routines and work out—

WOMAN THREE: I could do one of those aptitude tests that point out the important—

WOMAN ONE: You have to consider the full range of options—

WOMAN TWO: When you think of self-fulfillment and all that—

> *(Women exit still talking excitedly. Tape of music while women change. This scene is played with women wearing only their basic costumes accompanied by triple strings of pearls and small fur pieces. Their demeanor is of women fully and formally dressed. CLARA takes her place at a lectern, with a microphone if available, at stage right. Two other women, ALICE [EAST], and BUNNY [NORTH], sit at the card table, and fourth woman, FUR STOLE [SOUTH], wearing a fur stole over her shoulders, takes a seat in the front of the theatre. Lights on CLARA.)*

CLARA: *(Speaking from lectern.)* Good evening, ladies and gentlemen. It is my pleasure to introduce to you a group of ... friends, dear friends, who have been together for ... *(She consults her notes.)* for years and years. And years. Decades. What I mean to say is, generations. Yes, I know it's hard to believe, but this group has become a Tuesday night institution. A veritable institution. Together through a major depression, a world war, yes, way back then. Elections, spirals of affluence, miraculous inventions, death, illness, birth—*(Pauses, looks at notes.)* I did say death, didn't I? Well, I haven't come here tonight to bring gloom and doom, I'm here to present to you—and here they are—The Martha Circle!

(FUR STOLE applauds lustily from front row of theatre. Light goes up on card table.)

ALICE: *(Briskly dealing out four hands, she looks up in surprise, then begins to speak very rapidly.)* Oh! Hello there. My name is Alice Evans, longtime member of the Martha Circle, going back to ... since ... well, it feels like forever, I can't just ... quite remember when ... it must be twelve years now, something like that. I'd just moved here from Kenora and someone I ran into said, would I like to sub one night. It seemed one of the group, Geraldine her name was, who'd replaced someone called Ruth something-or-other from way back— well, this Geraldine person, she'd moved to the coast, reasons of health, asthma, and they needed a fourth. That first night, ha, I felt like I was on trial. I was pret-ty rusty, it'd been a few years since I'd picked up a deck of—*(Slows down.)* A funny thing—that first night I felt like I was in someone else's skin. Yeah. Not what you'd call a bad feeling, just like the way you feel, you know, when you maybe go down a long hallway and pop open the wrong door by mistake?—like you're all of a sudden in this different room where you hadn't in-tended to be?—But it doesn't seem to matter, if you see what I mean, it's like where you wanted to be ... *(Pause.)* all along sort of thing?

CLARA: Thank you so much, and now—*(Gestures at BUNNY.)*

BUNNY: *(Briskly.)* Right. How did I become a member of the Martha Circle? Well, I replaced Cora Fadden exactly two years ago. Cora, as everyone knows, was with the Royal Bank, still is as a matter of fact, and they asked her if she'd accept a transfer to Toronto. She hated like anything to go. She'd been a Martha Circle regular for, oh, I'd say seven or eight years. She took over, if I've got this straight, from a gal called Marcella Henry who fell out of a window, she was watering some geraniums, this huge big window box she had. Marcella, of course, replaced Doris Veal, one of the originals if I'm not mistaken. You might say I'm sort of the replacement for the replacement for the replacement—ha! Well, that's my story. Any questions?

CLARA: *(Into microphone.)* Yes, are there any questions?

FUR STOLE: *(Rising.)* I was just wondering, well, this is getting into ancient history, I suppose, but I was wondering what ever happened to Clara. *(Clears throat.)* Clara Wesley. *(Sits.)*

CLARA: *(After a long pause.)* Well, the fact is, maybe I should have said so in my introduction. I'm ... *I'm* Clara Wesley. I go right back to the

beginning. Doris Veal, Ruth Sprague, Margot Hetherling, and myself,
Clara Wesley. Except now, of course, it's Clara Hetherling.

FUR STOLE: Hetherling? What do you mean, Hetherling?

CLARA: Well, I thought everyone knew—you see, when Margot died
leaving Ronald—there I was. My poor Arthur had been gone for
years, and so he and I, Ronald and I—

FUR STOLE: —got together.

CLARA: Married, yes. He wanted me to take his name and I thought,
well, why not?—

FUR STOLE: *(Speaking very deliberately.)* So you replaced Wesley ...
with Hetherling?

CLARA: It took a little getting used to, but—

FUR STOLE: And then, I suppose, you moved into ... Margot
Hetherling's old house.

CLARA: It seemed the best idea, they had this almost new furnace, and
that wonderful deep backyard, and the rose bushes Margot'd put in,
and the lilacs—

FUR STOLE: And I imagine you ... you moved into Margot's old
bedroom too.

CLARA: Well—

FUR STOLE: Her own bed even.

CLARA: That did feel ... a little ... odd. At first. Sometimes I'd be lying
there and I'd start to think—these same sheets, this same blanket. I'd
think—Margot used to lie under this same blue woolen blanket, with
the same satin binding touching her lips—

FUR STOLE: And?

CLARA: And, well ... Ronald too, of course.

FUR STOLE: Yes, Ronald, of course.

CLARA: Sometimes ... there were moments ... well, perhaps I should
explain that Ronald ... took me by surprise ... in the beginning, that
is. He turned out to be a ... a ... a very romantic man. For his age. And
considering his background. Really quite ... very ... hmmm ...
passionate.

(All the women nod.)

Sometimes, I can't explain it, but I used to get the feeling, at those
moments ... I'd start to wonder if he wasn't maybe thinking about

Margot. Touching me, my … body—oh, he was gentle, oh my—but all the time thinking about Margot. I was sure he was thinking of her. I was positive. And I kept thinking, one of these … nights … he'll say it, say it out loud, her name … Margot.

FUR STOLE: And? Did it ever happen?

CLARA: No. It … didn't happen quite that way.

FUR STOLE: What then?

CLARA: It was me … one night. Instead of Ronald, it was me. I don't know what I was thinking. Well, I wasn't really thinking at all, I was, well, a long way off … *(Gives an embarrassed laugh.)* and it just came out of my mouth, sliding out on top of my breath somehow— Arthur. Just like that. Arthur, Arthur. Like a kind of cry. Like I was calling him back, only I wasn't, not really. Oh, I felt awful. I thought, oh, how I've hurt him, dear Ronald, how could I?

BUNNY: And what did he say?

CLARA: *(Rattled.)* Who?

ALICE: Ronald. What did Ronald say?

CLARA: *(Laughing a little.)* Well, he said … he said … now, Ronald was a passionate man, as I mentioned, almost … almost wild … at times … but he never said a great deal. Some people, you know, are like that.

FUR STOLE: *(Rising, approaching CLARA and letting the fur stole slide down.)* That's true enough. Some people are like that, not given to saying what they're feeling.

CLARA: But on this particular night, when I lost my head and came out with … well, there I was ready to die of shame, but Ronald, he—

(The four women take their places at the table and pick up their cards.)

But Ronald, he just held me … held me in his arms, oh so tight-like, and he said, "I love you, Clara." Hmmm. *(Remembering.)* He said, "I love you, my only, only Clara."

FUR STOLE: *(Folds stole over back of chair and holds out hand to be shaken.)* Angie Peterson. Filling in tonight for Rosie Elwood, she's in Hawaii.

(Women move to centre stage and gather around microphone. The following song, lyrics provisional, to be sung with a gospel rhythm and blues feel.)

Refrain:
>   Hands, hands, hands, hands, (do mi so do)
>   Thirteen hands, I got thirteen hands,
>   Thirteen hands waving at me,
>   Holding down the fam-i-ly tree.

>   *(With variations: "Holding firm to the fam-i-ly tree," "Counting
>   the twigs on the fam-i-ly tree," "Keeping track of the fam-i-ly
>   tree," "Propping up the fam-i-ly tree," "Singing 'round the fam-
>   i-ly tree.")*

Hands of diamonds, hands of clubs,
Hands rinsed rough in washing tubs,
Hands of hearts and hands of spades,
Hands whose girlish beauty fades.

Hands be-gloved, hands beloved,
Women's hands with wedding bands,
Hands that raise themselves in doubt,
Hands that count the money out
(dishing out the sauerkraut).

>   *(Refrain.)*

Shaping hands and knowing hands,
Crocheting hands and sewing hands,
Bedside hands and birthing hands,
Hands alight and cooling hands.

>   *(The following verse is recited.)*

Hands unkissed or in a fist,
Hands that salute the absolute,
Counting hands and praying hands,
Hands that take a public stand.

Hands that feed and hands that fill,
Hands at rest and hands grown still,
Hands that hammer, hands that hack,
Hands that hold the thunder back.

>   *(Refrain.)*

Erotic hands, exotic hands,
Traveling-round-the-worldly hands,
Caressing hands and blessing hands,
Ring-around-the-rosy hands.

Hands that reach and catch the rain.
Hands that take the sting from pain.
Wheeling, dealing, reeling, hands.

Hmmm mm mmm mmm (do me so do)
Thirteen hands, we need thirteen hands,
Hands held tight through thick and thin
(hey, make that thin and thick),
Hands held tight through thin and thick.
It takes thirteen tricks to make a hand,
And thirteen hands to do the trick.

(Women enter dressing room and change for next scene into tie-on skirts—micro-short, short, longer, and very long—that reflect their different ages: great-grandmother, grandmother, mother and daughter.

Stage is dark. Sound of loud creaking. Large shadows on the walls. Light comes up on CLARA, as a great-grandmother, in wheelchair entering from one side of stage; she stops and composes her hands; light comes up on Clara's DAUGHTER [EAST], sixty. Exaggerated sound of footsteps; two women, one about forty, Clara's GRANDDAUGHTER [NORTH], the other a teenager, Clara's GREAT-GRANDDAUGHTER [SOUTH], enter talking to each other.)

GRANDDAUGHTER: *(To GREAT-GRANDDAUGHTER.)* It'll just be an hour or so, I promise.

GREAT-GRANDDAUGHTER: A whole hour!

GRANDDAUGHTER: Shhhh. She'll hear you.

GREAT-GRANDDAUGHTER: You've got to be kidding. You'd have to put a bomb under her to—

GRANDDAUGHTER: Shhhh. She's got her new hearing a-i-d on.

DAUGHTER: *(To everyone, in a false-cheery voice.)* Isn't it wonderful! *(Wheels wheelchair up to card table.)* Granny Clara's got a new hearing aid.

GRANDDAUGHTER: Very attractive. Granny Clara. *(Louder.)* I said, it's very attractive.

CLARA: What?

GRANDDAUGHTER: I said it's very attractive.

CLARA: I heard you. *(Pause.)* What's attractive?

GREAT-GRANDDAUGHTER: *(Giving CLARA a kiss and shouting.)* Your hearing aid, Gran. Very nice.

CLARA: And what's so nice about it? *(Starts dealing out hands.)*

DAUGHTER: It's, it's not as, as noticeable as your old one.

GRANDDAUGHTER: The one you refused to wear.

GREAT-GRANDDAUGHTER: *(Whispering.)* The one you kept hiding in the cutlery drawer. Under the spoons.

CLARA: The moon? What about the moon?

DAUGHTER: We were just saying, there's a full moon tonight. The moon is made of blue cheese.

GREAT-GRANDDAUGHTER: Green cheese. The moon. That's what you always used to say, Mom.

GRANDDAUGHTER: *(Picking up hand.)* Did I? Two hearts.

CLARA: What was that?

DAUGHTER: Two hearts, Mother. Your bid.

CLARA: Two hearts?

GREAT-GRANDDAUGHTER: I can't stand this, we're never going to get done here. I've got this essay to finish and there's a movie on channel—

GRANDDAUGHTER: *(Whispering.)* One hour. Is that too much to ask? A few hands with your mother and grandmother.

DAUGHTER: And your great-grandmother. It does her the world of good. Keeps her alert.

GRANDDAUGHTER: Good therapy, best there is.

CLARA: Two spades.

DAUGHTER: Th—ree hearts. *(Louder.)* Three hearts.

GREAT-GRANDDAUGHTER: Four spades.

DAUGHTER: You only have to go to three, dear.

GREAT-GRANDDAUGHTER: Four.

GRANDDAUGHTER: Are you sure. You don't really have to …

CLARA: If she said four—

GRANDDAUGHTER: Pass.

CLARA: Five spades.

DAUGHTER: Five! Pass.

GREAT-GRANDDAUGHTER: Pass. And I mean pass. Do I ever mean pass.

GRANDDAUGHTER: Pass.

GREAT-GRANDDAUGHTER: We've had it. We've goofed, Granny Clara. We're into the primordial—

(Four women play the hand out as they talk.)

CLARA: I remember one night, oh, I think it was during the war, one night, summer, I think. Margot had just dealt out the nicest spade hand—

GREAT-GRANDDAUGHTER: Which war was this?

DAUGHTER: Shhhh.

GREAT-GRANDDAUGHTER: I've gotta do this essay about the treaty of Versailles and I was just wondering if maybe Grandma was there.

GRANDDAUGHTER: Trump.

DAUGHTER: Rot-ten split.

CLARA: It was toward the end of the war, not that we knew it was toward the end, how would we know that?

DAUGHTER: Another spade! I do not believe it.

CLARA: Everything was rationed, butter, sugar, the lot. Coffee even. We'd get together, Tuesday nights as usual, Doris, Margot, Ruth Sprague, and what'd we serve? A slice of Spam on a cracker *(Laughs.)* and we used to make this concoction called eggless chocolate cake. We'd put something in it to make it rise, what was it now?

GRANDDAUGHTER: Was it good?

CLARA: I can't remember. It didn't matter. We didn't think about it.

GREAT-GRANDDAUGHTER: *(Whispering.)* Well, you're thinking about it now.

GRANDDAUGHTER: Shhhh.

CLARA: Vinegar, I think. A couple of tablespoons of white vinegar—

DAUGHTER: Down one!

CLARA: There we were, 1944, or maybe 1943—I wish I could remember—

DAUGHTER: It doesn't matter, Mother.

CLARA: —Margot had just dealt out this beautiful hand, that is to say I had the most beautiful hand, a nice run of spades—and—my diamonds were pretty good too.

GREAT-GRANDDAUGHTER: I don't believe it, we did it, Gran, five spades. Hee! We actually made five spades. And the crowds go wild—

CLARA: —and all of a sudden Ruth Sprague, you remember, Ruth Sprague, dear—

(Dialogue from this point goes at top speed.)

DAUGHTER: As if I could forget. That wonderful black hair, the way she parted it down the middle and wore it in these coils over her ears. Like little earphones.

GREAT-GRANDDAUGHTER: There's this girl in my class, Rosalie Spiers, who wears her hair in—

DAUGHTER: Rosalie? Spiers? Would she be the one whose sister married the Hungarian labor organizer and went—

GREAT-GRANDDAUGHTER: Her cousin. Remember? The one with the thing on her forehead? Right in the middle of the forehead? Rosie's sister is the one who got so sunburned that time she had to—

DAUGHTER: Ruth Sprague, she really did have hair that—

CLARA: You're thinking of Doris, it was Doris Veal who had the—

DAUGHTER: That's right, Doris had the hair. And the Vauxhall. Her own car, and that was something in those days, a woman having her own car. Oh, I remember Doris Veal. I remember that uproar about her son—

GRANDDAUGHTER: —her grandson—

CLARA: Lovely boy—

GREAT-GRANDDAUGHTER: Teddy? Teddy Veal? The same one who got what's-her-name pregnant. Charlene Windsor.

DAUGHTER: They both sang in the same choir too. That's the whole point. Charlene Windsor's father, he voted Liberal—

GREAT-GRANDAUGHTER: —wasn't he the one—

GRANDDAUGHTER: —exactly. It was on Valentine's Day, he was courting Eleanor McMurtry who was related, very distantly of course, to—what was her name anyway?

CLARA: Geraldine. She had trouble with asthma, always did, more or less ran in the family. Judge McMurtry, you remember poor old Judge McMurtry—

DAUGHTER: They were cousins or something.

CLARA: By marriage only. I think it was Judge McMurtry who—

GRANDDAUGHTER: Do you mean the Judge McMurtry? I think you mean his half-brother, what was his name, Foster. Long bushy beard. Big black boots? Remember when he played Santa Claus for the Lions and his beard caught fire. Ed Kroger came running over with a fire extinguisher—

DAUGHTER: He was married three times, Ed Kroger, imagine, and he was not what I would call an attractive man either, and his third wife—was it Bessie?

CLARA: No, I don't think it was Bessie. Lizzy maybe.

DAUGHTER: Lizzy, she was the one, I'm sure she was, who had to have her gall bladder out while she was in Victoria attending a teachers' convention and her sister-in-law—

GRANDDAUGHTER: That would be Marguerite. I was a friend of hers before she married Bob Hartley, his mother was Doris Veal's cousin, the one who married the youngest Spicer boy—his sister married into the Hartwells. It was his brother, Grover Spicer who beat his wife and went to jail for it and later converted to Catholicism, remember that priest, Father What's-his-name, came from Quebec and spoke with that—where was I?—Marguerite, this will amaze you but Marguerite got the silver medal the year we graduated, she had these pathetic bowed legs—

CLARA: That was the polio. Her mother was in a state—

DAUGHTER: Never the same after—

CLARA: True.

GRANDDAUGHTER: Sad.

DAUGHTER: Tragic.

CLARA: Couldn't be helped, of course. Not in those days.

GRANDDAUGHTER: Not with that family background. Her uncle—

CLARA: He was, well this was later, he was—what's the word?

DAUGHTER: Eccentric. Ha. He had himself a permanent wave, yes, really, a perm, and he wore cologne. Evening in Paris if I'm not mistaken—

GREAT-GRANDDAUGHTER: Was he the guy they found in the park with the fishing rod and the sack of oranges and the—?

CLARA: No, that was Myron Bell. His mother and my mother went to school together. She was an Ambrose, fine family, St. George's, very active, but they did things differently, that family. We used to say it was because they were from Newfoundland.

DAUGHTER: *(Musing.)* But aren't we all? From Newfoundland. Metaphorically, I mean.

CLARA: Just to give you a for instance, they believed in using their silver every day, sterling silver, and then she married a Bell, one of the Selkirk Bells, and that was the end of the silver—all of it got sold—and the start of, what was it now? Nine children, ten maybe. This was before the days of—Myron was the last of the lot, a strange child. He talked to animals, birds and so on. So the episode in the park didn't really surprise us.

GREAT-GRANDDAUGHTER: Is it true he took his fishing rod and the—

GRANDDAUGHTER: Good heavens, now how do you know about Myron Bell in the park with the oranges and the fishing rod. You weren't even born then.

DAUGHTER: You weren't born either. And don't forget the grapefruit. What he did with the grapefruit.

GRANDDAUGHTER: That's right. And I haven't forgotten the grapefruit, how could I?

(All four laugh hysterically.)

DAUGHTER: I guess it's history more or less. Real history!

GREAT-GRANDDAUGHTER: This essay I'm writing—

CLARA: And so ... on this night, I remember it as though it were ... minutes ago ... Ruth Sprague looked at her hand, these lovely spades and said right out loud ... now, what was it she said?

(There is a long pause.)

DAUGHTER: You feel up to another hand, Mother?

CLARA: I wish I could remember things. Not everything, but I wish I could remember what we talked about all those years. Margot and Ruth and Doris and—

GRANDDAUGHTER: Whose deal is it? I've lost track.

DAUGHTER: Yours, I think.

GREAT-GRANDDAUGHTER: Gossip.

GRANDDAUGHTER: *(Sharply.)* Gossip? What do you mean, gossip?

GREAT-GRANDDAUGHTER: Well, Granny Clara was wondering ... what she and her cronies used to—

GRANDDAUGHTER: Oh, they weren't cronies, cronies isn't the word, they were—

DAUGHTER: It wasn't really gossip, not the way you're thinking of.

GREAT-GRANDDAUGHTER: *(Shouting.)* What'd ya talk about, Gran, if you weren't dishing the dirt? Your old boy friends? Your beaux?

CLARA: No, I don't think so, I don't remember—

GRANDDAUGHTER: Your husbands probably. Your hubbies and your kids.

CLARA: Well, maybe now and then, but—

DAUGHTER: What you were gonna fix for dinner. Recipes.

CLARA: I suppose we did. From time to time, but most of the time— now I remember! What we talked about. *(Pause.)* We talked about our mothers.

> *(Lights dim. Tape of women talking and laughing. Fade. Lights come up immediately on CLARA at centre of darkened stage in wheelchair. She rises suddenly to her feet, facing audience directly.)*

> *(Repeating in exactly the same tone she used previously.)* Now I remember. We talked about our mothers.

> *(While CLARA listens, other women speak from various positions on stage.)*

WOMAN TWO [EAST]: My mother, she used to put thirteen egg whites in a cake. The recipe called for twelve, but, no, that wouldn't do, she always put in thirteen—for good luck, she said.

WOMAN THREE [SOUTH]: Not my mother, no siree, if it called for twelve eggs, she put in eleven. Waste not, want not—

WOMAN FOUR [NORTH]: Well, when it came to children, bringing them up, my mother had this saying. One is one, she said, but two is ten. That's a kind of proverb, I think. Icelandic. Or else she made it up, she was like that—

WOMAN THREE: When bad things happened, sickness, death, tragedy, she used to say—oh, she knew her bible backwards and forwards— she used to say—tares among the wheat, tares among the wheat—

WOMAN FOUR: Become a nun, she said, and you get none. Ha.

WOMAN THREE: A mother needs a dozen eyes and thirteen hands, that's what my mother used to say—

WOMAN TWO: Of course she always called my father "her better half." But the way she said it, her tone of voice, it was, like a private joke she had—like she was sucking on a pickle.

WOMAN FOUR: Shabby underwear, she'd say, is the sign of a shabby—

WOMAN TWO: Never skimp on baking chocolate. Or good wool gloves or—

WOMAN THREE: —there she'd be out in the back garden. Early in the morning. She loved the early morning, especially in the summertime. She'd be out there picking raspberries, she'd have a whole bowl picked by the time the rest of us—

WOMAN TWO: Indisposed, she used to say. Or my granny's come calling. Or I fell off the roof. Well, we knew what that meant.

WOMAN FOUR: —of course she was ex-communicated when she married, but sometimes we'd catch her, standing at the window, making the sign of the cross—

WOMAN THREE: —that's what she said. She said it only once, but it … *(Pause.)* stuck with me. That she'd wanted to be an opera singer when she was a girl, go away to Europe and have her voice trained. And she couldn't carry a tune in a basket.

WOMAN FOUR: —my father used to say it shamed him, seeing her chop kindling, but she loved it, loved getting outdoors—

WOMAN TWO: —well, they didn't have running water, but she had this saying, "A lady can take a bath in a teacup." And she could—

WOMAN THREE: —mysterious aches and pains especially in her legs. Of course the doctors didn't know anything then about—

WOMAN TWO: —hid in the closet during the electric storms. She used to take us with her, we could feel her trembling in the dark.

WOMAN FOUR: Well, when there was thunder, she'd say, "It's just the angels moving their furniture." Her voice bright as—

WOMAN TWO: She'd launch into this story about her cousin Aaron, struck by lightening, standing there between the house and barn. The tears would roll down her face. And this happened maybe fifty years back.

WOMAN THREE: She smacked us on the back of the hand. Hard. With anything she happened to have in her hand, a wooden spoon, whatever. Her mean streak. We learned to keep out of her way when she was in one of her moods.

WOMAN TWO: —used to say how her idea of paradise was sitting in front of the wood stove with her feet up on a chair, she had this problem with her veins, her mother had had the same thing, and now I—

WOMAN FOUR: —my father's shirts. It's the least I can do for him, she used to say, send him out in the world every day with a properly ironed shirt and collar.

WOMAN THREE: *(Counting on fingers.)*—never rode a bicycle, never went ice-skating, not once, never had a real engagement ring—

WOMAN TWO: Well, you know how it was then, spring cleaning began the first day of April, but she liked to get a head start. She'd get my father to carry out the carpets—there'd be snow on the bushes but she'd get going. It was like a *(Harshly.)* sickness she had.

WOMAN FOUR: —saved every letter and post card she ever got, she had boxes and boxes of them, and after she died we found—

WOMAN TWO: —saved wrapping paper, string, she even saved her basting threads and used them over again.

WOMAN FOUR: —hoarded the little stumpy ends of candles, saved orange peels to make candy out of—

WOMAN TWO: —saved this post card of Niagara Falls where—

WOMAN THREE: —saved a lock of my father's hair, from when he was a young man?—courting, smitten to the heart, and years later when he was bald as a—well, she'd show us kids this little piece of hair, tender like a baby's hair, she had it all tied up with a bitty piece of ribbon, she'd get it out and show it to us and say, "Your father, he was a prince."

WOMAN TWO: Oh, oh, she started one night—coughing up blood—

(WOMAN TWO rises from the table and moves toward bicycle.)

WOMAN THREE: —a tumor in her stomach the size of two fists—

WOMAN FOUR: —broken hip, her bones were like finest china. Shattered. Oh, dear God, that was the beginning of the end—

(A change of light indicates a change of mood. SCARF [EAST], mounted on bicycle, approaches CLARA, ringing bell, she has tied a scarf around her head.)

SCARF [EAST]: *(She is not so much angry as emotionally on edge, close to tears.)* Pardon me. Pardon me? It's none of my business, but, I wonder, has it ever occurred to you that you could have been knitting wool socks for our fighting men, the four of you? Did you ever stop to think of that? You could have been rolling bandages. But, no, there you were, playing hand after hand every Tuesday night when our Christian missions in Africa and China were begging for flannel nightgowns and bibles and warm blankets. You could have saved lives. Yes, you could have. You could have been—useful.

CLARA: *(Taken back.)* Well, the fact is ... you see ... we never thought—we felt we needed a little—

SCARF: *(Tearful.)* At least, at least you might have talked about something interesting? The history of the Commonwealth? Russian novels? Medieval art? Now that's a very interesting subject, medieval art. You could have been learning a foreign language on those Tuesday nights. You could have looked into philosophy, economics, investment opportunities. Oh, there were so many useful—

CLARA: *(Wonderingly.)* Investment opportunities?

SCARF: Or you could have been, you know, out fighting for political change, for the extension of women's rights. You could have bettered your conditions, enriched your lives. Do you know what?—you could have ... you could have made something of yourselves.

CLARA: It was ... not at our disposal, we did not have at our disposal—

SCARF: How could you have thrown away all that time.

CLARA: *(Merrily.)* I don't know ... but we did.

SCARF: And there's one thing I'll never be able to understand.

CLARA: Why, I know you, you're Doris Veal's oldest girl.

SCARF: Remember how at the funeral you came up to me, all teary-eyed—oh, it made me sick—and said you felt like you'd lost a sister.

CLARA: She was. We were all of us—

SCARF: Oh, when I think about it. Those Tuesday nights of yours. Sitting there. The blue rinse girls. The white-glove ladies. Shuffling cards. Killing time. Running away from reality.

CLARA: Well, reality now, that's a good point. Who knows what it really is. It's a *funny* thing. Sometimes it—reality I'm talking about—shrinks down so small it's no bigger than that card table over there.

SCARF: I can tell you about reality if you want.

CLARA: You see, we thought—

SCARF: My mother, your friend Doris Veal, was sober one day out of the week, Tuesday. On Tuesday she got up sober and went to bed sober—so she'd be fit to go to Martha Circle. The rest of the time, well. It went on for years. You could have done something, helped her. But you didn't even know.

CLARA: That's not—true.

SCARF: None of you lifted a finger. You didn't do one thing.

CLARA: I can't tell you—we wanted more than anything—

SCARF: You turned a blind eye. *(Voice breaking.)*

CLARA: Yes. *(Slowly.)* A blind eye. I suppose you could call it that.

SCARF: You just let her be. Just let her *(Pause.)* be.

CLARA: *(Softly.)* That's what we did. Yes.

SCARF: You let her be.

> *(Her voice breaks. The two women take each other's hands, an open embrace of understanding.)*

CLARA: *(Pulling away.)* And, you know, sitting there, the four of us, we were as close together as people can get.

SCARF: Close.

CLARA: When people think about being close, they think of two people in bed together, a husband and wife, a man and a woman, but this was closer. At that card table we were closer, you know, than families are sitting at a dining table, sitting with your own flesh and blood, eating a Sunday dinner. I'm talking about inches away, real distance as we measure it.

SCARF: And the things you talked about—

CLARA: It was as if our brains were so busy, counting points, planning the next move, trying to guess what was in our partner's head, and you know, we got so we could do just that, it was like a kind of enchantment—well, there we were, thinking so hard about what we were doing that our tongues just went and did what they wanted to do, said things that seemed to come out of nowhere, came right up out of foreign parts of us. Oh, it was a strange thing, those cards slipping out of one hand into another.

> *(SCARF nodding, understanding.)*

It was like we were making something, a kind of handiwork, and everything else falling away. It was like a little planet we'd put together and it was us who'd written the rules and bought the furniture and the curtains and the carpets and we'd set it whirling out there in the darkness. At that table, I knew exactly where I was.

SCARF: *(Quietly.)* And where exactly *(Pause.)* were you—?

CLARA: I was ... I don't know ... at home! At home in the world. Ruth. Margot. Doris. Oh my, the four of us around that table, dealing out hands. I know it's hard to believe, but we were young then. Young ... as ... girls! Starting out our lives. Every Tuesday night. We couldn't see into the future, of course we couldn't. The future was too far away. But we could see as far as Tuesday night. And that was enough. We'd get together in each other's houses, those little living rooms, all dusted, the table set up, everything ready. *(Expository tone.)* On Tuesdays, for once, we'd leave the dishes in the sink. We'd try to start as soon after supper as we could get away, oh, I'd say about seven-thirty or thereabouts, it would just be getting dark, twilight—

> *(Clarinet music. Lights fade, then up again in the form of flickering silent-movie lighting. Clarinet music fades to nickelodeon music. A young woman wearing a vaguely twenties outfit carries on stage a flip chart or electronic substitute if possible, on which are written the titles that accompany the silent film sequence which follows. The first title reads "The Card Party," and she immediately flips this so that the card reads, "Waiting for Clara." She is joined by two others, similarly dressed. The three of them go to an imaginary window, gesturing broadly. One returns to flip chart, and turns leaf to reveal the title: "Where, oh, where is Clara?"*
>
> *The three women gesture broadly at each other, shrugging, questioning. Nickelodeon music grows louder. They go again to the window and look out. One goes to chart and turns to next title: "This is very mysterious." One woman rushes off stage and returns with tea tray; she mimes an offer of tea, but the others shake their heads.*
>
> *The three women sit at table: one holds up deck of cards: all look agitated. One goes to flip chart and turns to "Where, oh where is Clara?" and flips immediately to next title which says: "What can be keeping her?"*
>
> *One woman goes to window again. She peers out and begins to mime wildly. Other women run to window, gesturing wildly, then run to flip chart revealing "At last."*
>
> *The young CLARA enters, running from stage left: the others embrace her and lead her to table. They sit at table, pick up cards.*

A warm, golden, steady light replaces black and white film flicker; nickelodeon music fades to recorded music. Women freeze. Light slowly fades. Very gradual introduction of tape of women talking and laughing.

The end.)

Plays available from Blizzard Publishing

❑ *Amigo's Blue Guitar*, MacLeod, J.
  $10.95 (pb) 0-921368-23-2

❑ *Beautiful Lake Winnipeg*, Hunter, M.
  $10.95 (pb) 0-921368-10-0

❑ *Bordertown Café*, Rebar, K.
  $10.95 (pb) 0-921368-08-9

❑ *Castrato*, Nelson, G.
  $11.95 (pb) 0-921368-31-3

❑ *Chinese Man Said Goodbye, The*,
  McManus, B.
  $10.95 (pb) 0-921368-05-4

❑ *Darling Family, The: A Duet for Three*,
  Griffiths, L.
  $10.95 (pb) 0-921368-17-8

❑ *Democracy*, Murrell, J.
  $10.95 (pb) 0-921368-28-3

❑ *Departures and Arrivals*, Shields, C.
  $10.95 (pb) 0-921368-13-5

❑ *Exile*, Crail, A.
  $10.95 (pb) 0-921368-12-7

❑ *Fire*, Ledoux, P. & Young, D.
  $9.95 (pb) 0-929091-05-1

❑ *Footprints On the Moon*, Hunter, M.
  $10.95 (pb) 0-921368-07-0

❑ *Gravel Run*, Massing, C.
  $10.95 (pb) 0-921368-16-X

❑ *Invention of Poetry, The*, Quarrington, P.
  $9.95 (pb) 0-929091-31-0

❑ *Mail Order Bride, The*, Clinton, R.
  $10.95 (pb) 0-921368-09-7

❑ *Memories of You*, Lill, W.
  $9.95 (pb) 0-929091-06-X

❑ *Midnight Madness*, Carley, D.
  $9.95 (pb) 0-920197-88-4

❑ *Mirror Game*, Foon, D.
  $10.95 (pb) 0-921368-24-0

❑ *Oldest Living, The*, Smith, P.
  $5.95 (pb) 0-920999-02-6

❑ *Particular Class of Women, A*, Feindel, J.
  $7.95 (pb) 0-920999-10-7

❑ *Prairie Report*, Moher, F.
  $10.95 (pb) 0-921368-15-1

❑ *refugees*, Rintoul, H.
  $7.95 (pb) 0-921368-02-X

❑ *Sky*, Gault, C.
  $10.95 (pb) 0-921368-06-2

❑ *Soft Eclipse, The*, Gault, C.
  $10.95 (pb) 0-921368-14-3

❑ *Steel Kiss*, Fulford, R.
  $10.95 (pb) 0-921368-19-4

❑ *Third Ascent, The*, Moher, F.
  $10.95 (pb) 0-921368-04-6

❑ *Thirteen Hands*, Shields, C.
  $11.95 (pb) 0-921368-30-5

❑ *Transit of Venus*, Hunter, M.
  $10.95 (pb) 0-921368-29-1

❑ *Unidentified Human Remains and the
  True Nature of Love*, Fraser, B.
  $10.95 (pb) 0-921368-11-9

❑ *Writing With Our Feet*, Carley, D.
  $10.95 (pb) 0-921368-20-8

Anthologies

❑ *Adventures for (Big) Girls: Seven Radio
  Plays*, Jansen, A. (Ed.)
  $16.95 (pb) 0-921368-32-1

❑ *Airborne: Radio Plays by Women*,
  Jansen, A. (Ed.)
  $14.95 (pb) 0-921368-22-4

❑ *Dangerous Traditions: A Passe Muraille
  Anthology*, Rudakoff, J. (Ed.)
  $19.95 (pb) 0-921368-27-5

❑ *Endangered Species: Four Plays*,
  Hollingsworth, M.
  $10.95 (pb) 0-9693639-0-1

Anthologies (cont.)

❑ *On the MAP: Scenes Workshopped by the Manitoba Playwrights Development Program,* Runnells, R. (Ed.)
$11.95 (pb) 0-9693890-0-0

❑ *Take Five: The Morningside Dramas,* Carley, D. (Ed.)
$14.95 (pb) 0-921368-21-6

Theatre Studies

❑ *Dramatic Body, The: A Guide to Physical Characterization,* Jetsmark, T. (trans. P. Brask)
$15.95 (pb) 0-921368-25-9

❑ *Hot Ice: Shakespeare in Moscow, A Director's Diary,* Sprung, G. (with R. Much)
$15.95 (pb) 0-921368-18-6

❑ *Women on the Canadian Stage: The Legacy of Hrotsvit,* Much, R. (Ed.)
$16.95 (pb) 0-921368-26-7

To Order:

BLIZZARD PUBLISHING

301 - 89 Princess St., Winnipeg, MB
CANADA R3B 1K6

Please send me the titles I have indicated:

Name: ....

Address: ....

City: ....State/Prov.: ....Code: ....

Please send cheque or money order; no cash or C.O.D.
Add $1.50 for shipping; or 50¢ per book for orders of more than five books.
Canadian residents add 7% GST. Allow three weeks for delivery.

❑ Free catalogues available on request.